IMPERIAL PHYSIQUE

Fig. 1. Hieronymus Bosch, *Ship of Fools* (1490–1500)

First published in 2019 by punctum books, Earth, Milky Way.
https://punctumbooks.com

ISBN-13: 978-1-950192-53-3 (print)
ISBN-13: 978-1-950192-54-0 (ePDF)

DOI: 10.21983/P3.0268.1.00

LCCN: 2019953098
Library of Congress Cataloging Data is available from the Library of Congress

Book design: Vincent W.J. van Gerven Oei
Cover image: Zach Grear, *Delirium* (2019). Courtesy of the artist.

The author and publisher have done their utmost best to seek reproduction permission from all copyright holders of the image materials included in this publication. Please contact the publisher with any further queries.

HIC SVNT MONSTRA

JH Phrydas

IMPERIAL PHYSIQUE

Contents

Acknowledgments

This book emerged through conversations across disciplines while I was a grad student at Naropa University: with Michael Franklin, who brought me into the world of clay, longitudinal embodiment, and offered me the honor of being the writer-in-residence at the Naropa Community Arts Center working with differently abled adults — who taught me so much about non-normative, non-ableist methods of communicating and connecting outside of verbal language; with Christine Caldwell, who explored the teachings of somatic psychology with me while I searched for ways to write about the infectiousness of queerness within nonverbal exchanges — anti-capitalist, pro-wild; and, Bhanu Kapil, without whom I would not be a writer, whose wisdom and deep discussions into my own childhood memories of mud and violence and Georgia red clay brought me to these interdisciplinary conversations in the first place, whose work on anti-colonial syntax embedded within me hope for livable futures, ones we can create through hard work for no one but ourselves and those that desperately need the worlds we might be a part in building. I love you all.

I also wish to thank the journals and presses who have published portions of this manuscript: Fact-Simile, for publishing "The Delusion Artist" (under the title "Homo Oeconomicos: A Sentence") in its print magazine *Fact-Simile* 10 (2014), and Essay Press, for publishing "Preface," "The Elusion Artist," and "Wild Horses of Mourning" as a chapbook in their EP series titled

Empire in Shade (2017). I wish to express deep gratitude to the artists and studios who have graciously allowed me to include reproductions of artworks for this book. This includes Willem ter Velde and Jolie van Leeuwen at archive Studio Dumas, Simonetta Torrini at Società Italiana degli Autori ed Editori, Dan Trujillo at Artist Rights Society, and EJ at ZIN Studio. Special thanks to Zach Grear for his gorgeous line drawing that graces the cover of this book.

For Bhanu

my body, being anyone's, a blank repeating his already

—Rob Halpern, *Music for Porn*

They were under the beech. Their clothes were damp and their feet frozen. They sank into a sodden earth.
`

—Jean Genet, *Funeral Rites*

PREFACE

Do you heed the imperial decree
to use your body to promote
good citizenry?

THE CITY IS ASLEEP, and the parks are dimly lit. The first thing I notice is a type of circling: sweat in night's heat. Silhouettes of bodies in the trees, on a park bench, leaning against lamp posts. This writing emerges from this heat. I was interested in cruising as a ritual: repeated over and over across the world. These days, dating apps have replaced open-air cruising in many ways. What was once a heavy presence in city parks has now been relegated to the virtual and domestic space: the dorm, apartment couch, or halogen-lit bathroom. The contemporary cruise, made more efficient and effortless, is now the "looking?" or "sup?" smart-phone conversation: physical contact initiated or rebuked with a nude selfie.

CRUISING IS NOT DEAD, though. Out in the open, yet secretly, people convene in public spaces both urban and along the outskirts of civic infrastructure. Here, words are hardly used. It is in the turn of a head; repeated eye contact; a shift of a hand toward the thigh that signals desire. This silent and subtle ritual is nonverbal. A physical call-and-response system toward and away from a touch many deem unholy. The body speaks for itself. Muscle, skin, posture, and facial expressions combine to communicate: yes, no, I want you, keep your distance, and in this silent dance, societal marks — such as class, money, and status — dissipate in the lamplight. As physical movements become the basis for acceptance or rejection, certain re-inscriptions of oppression remain — cruising does not, by any means, open up a space of utopian free-for-all. However, the index of bodies within public spaces creates micro-scenarios of choice: out of these bodies, which will I pursue? On the outskirts of economic regulation, late in the evening, away from the major avenues and wide sidewalks of urban commerce, bodies shed in order to open toward a lone stranger.

AND YET, this ritual is not just relegated to parks, abandoned shipyards, alleyways: unspoken gestures occur in broad daylight, on the subway car, in a grocery store, at the gym, in a museum. What cruising does is electrify this sequence of movements, elevating body positions to the point of pure pleasure, even when apprehension is secondary to the thrill of anticipation. Queer or otherwise, everyone is implicated in this silent rite: it is part of our species's imperative. And those that proactively seek it? In cities and interstate rest stops, one enters the space of cruising by becoming, in effect, a useless body — in wait for a synchronic indication. And yet, waiting implies *something to come*: a prescription filled at the city's public hospital; a bus ride to the beach; the bloom of California poppies along coastal rocks. There is nothing to fear in one who waits, since the hope of production tethers them to a future act. The unpredictable lies in loitering: our animal body allowed to stand idly, without apparent purpose. Someone passively regarding color and sound is improper and seems suspect — especially for certain bodies (black, brown, immigrant, homeless) for whom loitering is often seen as an illegal or unethical act. "I would join you in cruising Elysian Park," my friend told me, "but if caught, you'd get a ticket. I'd get deported."

Meanwhile, he wastes time along paths with frequent pauses. She leans against the brick wall for hours. They crouch in the shade of the magnolia trees without a cigarette to give them at least a semblance of productivity and thus good citizenry, of participating in the economic structure of things. Non-productive, the body enters the space between city and wildness, human and animal, scanning the landscape for any slight movement.

YEARS AGO, Stanley Frank and I were drinking Jameson at the Stud, a gay bar in San Francisco. The crowd hemmed us in along the wooden counter. I remember an intense muscle-smell and a sea of bare shoulders. Strobe lights lit dancing bodies and left corners dark, without contour. In the red pulse, he turned to me and said: "All anyone wants to do is sniff each other's butts, but we can't, and this," gesturing to the crowd, "is our coping mechanism."

And we cope. Of course, scientists can and will study the effects of pheromones, body type, hair patterns, the relative size of appendages and their subsequent relation to evolutionary characteristics, supreme adaptations, and the strength of genetic lineage. Some, however, know that when allowing desire to exist outside of Darwinian progressivism — always bent on advancement and health — sexual drive is far messier than a mechanism to purify and strengthen the species as a future organism. A loitering desire — non-productive — has rawer directives. In high school, I met a young woman at the Majestic Diner in Atlanta who told me: "I fuck everyone I meet to get to know them. It's easier to know if you should be friends once you find out how your bodies feel together." Another friend, years later in SF, gestured to a man across the room and said: "He shakes hands with his dick."

It's messy, I know — it can't not be — but might we lean toward a potentially more candid topology that prioritizes our bodies and how they interact? What is at stake in positioning ourselves as animal — wild — when safety, or lack thereof, is an inherent force of carnality? What are the politics of a visceral life? Does cruising bring about the destruction of religiously and politically sanctioned notions of decency — self-worth — the social bond of our moral and ethical requirement? Can we cruise and, in the circling, dissolve structes that ensnare us?

THESE STORIES AND ESSAYS revolve around the loiterer: the way the city and the park, a doubled body, temporally displaced, resonate at each breath in the space of anticipation — one usually thought of as breathless. Back against the tree, each attempt failing and begun again. On repeat, night after night. And I found myself writing, night after night, instead of wandering the parks and alleyways, these stories. Maybe there are more waiting to be written, like the tree-leaning body: "Write me," they say. "Come to the page and write me."

I began to explore what is unsaid within a language that seems to reject that silence. How does gestural desire — these silent bodies interacting in urban and wild settings — emerge, arise, cause shifts of perception, potential differences in how we think, what we feel — in effect, raising the question: what drives us?

Like the figure in the woods, writing demands a type of passivity. Do you feel it as you read? Reading, itself, is a sensual act, as sensations, body narrative, and the position of the author as they write emerges through the rise and fall of the breath of the line. Is it me or a character that wanders into the wild? Can you feel the wind against his skin, your skin? Do these words make your heart beat with the rhythm of the sentence?

Reading is a type of cruise: ritualized, repeated, we enter into books — and for what purpose but to make some sort of contact — a caress?

IMPERIAL PHYSIQUE

My love of Genet, in retaliation for your torment.
Your enemies, too, are mine —

LINGERING WILD

To make sense of a blood-drenched beginning...

- In the beginning, there is nothing. Only void. An animal creeps along a brushed, white path near rocks removed for the purpose of routing. Scent-made. These — the origin of trails — become easements of their own and are called logical. What is the logic of a smell? Tiny pores, when open, allow air to infiltrate and conform to spaces now occupied. Sharpened, the animal knows to turn left. The soil gives. Even a ground covered in small frozen leaves glows similarly, as if in levitation, projected from loam to the canopy overhead.

- Laid in patterns, "animal" is replaced by "individual," later, "individual" by "group." At some point, we begin to amass along avenues inherited without prior knowledge of the land and its ancestry. The animal waits as we pass — breathing.

- Along this land.

- Where wilderness lingers.

- Do you notice the city first beyond the brush? Or the forest first beyond the ridge of rooflines? Both presuppose a city

Moan.

stroke
you ~~fuck~~ the body to find its language

dissect

you splay the·body to find its forms

every body radia

whose forest exists at an edge or boundary; a secure distance. Imagine, instead, a city built *in* the forest — no building tall enough to penetrate the canopy. Would you feel more or less exposed here, where sidewalks blend under foliage lit from beneath by streetlamps?

- Every body yields:

- And it's in the yield that you open — abreast, an invitation — the curl of skin around a fingernail or a trail along the hedgerows.

- The within is auxiliary.

- If the forest is the city, and the city forest, fences are superfluous. Yet, granite evokes a similar response, molding a curve as they obtrude from the surface. The subtlety of outcropping forms inflects an even more powerful hold at the edge of trees where the grey of sidewalk joins dirt without effort. Because concrete, when ending, knows nothing of the earth continuing underneath.

- *To mark* comes from the term *boundary* but also *forest*. We mark the limits of a land and extract meaning, territories, and trace small tracts for ownership. To offset the tendency to stray, posts and carvings act as guides: boundary stones, marksmen's cautionary impressions. Beyond this, the margin: wildness and the sea.

- They built the city on soil too soft for foundation, red like clay, and the big-housed ones, when strolling, refrain from idle gazes. Stiff, they pass by tiny cafés, the street once covered with boot prints and dull ash, a violence in reverberation held deep within the soil. Marching tamped down the loose earth, once, like a thousand bloodied bodies in a heap: each face an occasion for color to surface under the water oak.

- They called this place *terminus* before a man arrived and claimed it as his own. His own, and then a daughter's. A daughter's, and then the sea's.

- We enter this forest *without ever having left it*: moisture, swamp heat and sinew, roots twining underfoot as our hands become wet. In time, each file shifts into place, thin strips of bark along magnetic fields. A building rises toward the limbs of trees. Between, a damp remainder — echoes of running horses — a muffled cry. And the crowd, en masse, pulls the rope taut.

- I can't help but watch the undulation of each pale denial caught in heaves that disappear along the horizon. Trees rise and obfuscate and calmly begin to settle along a low mist. Notice how the ridge flattens to the left, almost in waving, a sloping invitation to *go ahead, unearth.*

- Some draw lips back to smell the dampness underneath the matted leaves, a driving warmth. The hills solicit each of us to lie, and argil, molding to our silhouette, knows contour in advance. Because our bodies aren't the first. A promise, tuning its rhythm to our own.

- These rhythms breathe in a stretch of grass along the field and contract at the pouring of pitch and the process of evening. Wooden shacks dot the roads along the periphery where country store barrels overflow with taffy. Shelves filled with wooden games and bottled sodas, while outside, broken windows lean against the siding. Piles of red earth line ponds filled with giant turtles some catch in preparation for a Sunday stew. Beyond, the newly tarred road glitters with splintered bone.

- On the other side of the city, a scattering of small buildings congregates along the tree line. Old enough to remember how shoulders steam. Below, a cover of soft pine needles the earth.

- Here, cloth might be the closest metaphor since the city needs weft and weave to pattern. The suburbs cannot penetrate the pockets of people torn here and replanted and retorn and again and so colors rise and vibrate and clash. Descendants cause the big-housed one's anxiety, sweat forming in defense. Discharge is quick and leaves no scar. It maps and ventriloquizes them each into saying "this time, it's something I ate and not…*this place.*"

- We long for the need to examine the wild's edge where, beyond, child-sized animals crouch and wait.

- Vision proves touch; sensation, presence. A twitch among the shrubbery. A sound — a thrush.

- To breathe, we must slough off rough concrete, meadows yoked to blacktop as elm and dogwood watch in an ochre flurry. In evening light, systems appear. Neon lines map interior shifts where uneven bark leaves impressions on skin. The boundary between city and forest we want dissolved. Where language emerged to mark matter into mud.

- It's counterpoint: kudzu along the lintel.

- I allow vines to grow over my doorframe — an intention to perform the forest in the city when the limits are horizontally skewed toward a history of slaughter. The line between trees and sky hides clusters of dull green. Taking stock, we're required to spatially orient with each step. To tense muscles and scan; to tense muscles and re-scan; like this, until you reach home, leaving the city at your back to administer at will.

- Walking under constant shade, I attempt to retain a sense of me with an impossible, almost futuristic hunger. And yet, words fail to shift meaning in such exchange — a slight gesture — a bent leg. The wild exposes a sudden refusal to allow the back and forth of eyes — acts of compulsion. A desire to acquiesce.

- The how-to guide on cruising on blood-soaked land.

- Does containing a wilderness change its name? In a peripheral field, haze takes the form of minor bodies. A rock from which a metal rod protrudes anchors the scene. Heat moves likewise, a sweet dialogue amid a fringe of magnolia while someone dallies as if collecting sap.

- Maps are drawn with simple leg movements. A straggler only need rest beside a fence and take note.

- The sidewalk leans forward in an uneasy pitch.

- Subtle agitations drape like threads woven at the city's limit. Where blacktop crumbles into bits of teeth, finger bone, and nail. Silent, we twine root systems along rock walls — useless: inoperable and knotted at the ends. *This* the city tells us. To shield the big-housed ones from flashback paranoia.

- We recognize these knots not through faces or clothing but reassembled movements: positions, dances. Stiff odor tilts just as much as ritualized breathing. Bodies in heat while, just beyond, sidewalks reappear among footprints and the echo of streetcars. Little glows of lamps, floating orbs like midnight flowers surveilling such intricate elaborations.

- Hiding enacts the hunt, while looping remains pivotal. To track sensation, witness how fiddlehead ferns cover the bank under tulip poplar and loblolly pine. Where roads mask trails

(warm the air to contain
the trajectory of sound)

~~communion~~
~~from skin~~

~~+ failure~~)
~~hesitation~~)
~~cement~~)
~~hair~~)
~~underground~~)
~~ting~~

~~it is a closed space, close enough for an~~
~~other's air to breathe across your cheek,~~
~~where movement unfelt inspires~~
~~perspiration, sticking in its place after the~~
~~body is gone.~~ a minute gesture leaves its
mark, ~~a~~ small spot of unknown odor,
clinging moisture on your shirt, ~~or heavy~~
~~shorts.~~   the
      nevs
       of a

~~breathing is proof~~)
~~~ life~~

fluid begs for erosi

~ body opaque ~
transparency of admission

salt smell

eding,] ~
              cracking in dry heat

that bend along the riverbed. The pulse of crickets bridges and breaks harmony, each small gesture an invitation to stay.

- This rut, a line pressed into soil, an escape route: the soil-piled sides — fountains of stone — higher than eye-level. A ledge to survey the landscape still secluded from above.

- Strangers convene along these routes in view of a meadow or abandoned city plot ringed with a fence. We come together, aware that buildings and trees are not synonymous but retain causal relation; one, and then the other, and then the one, infinitely.

- *Bewilder*: to lead astray; to lead into the forest; to lead into the wild.

- Some of us remain indoors, while others take backroads under cement overpasses. Out from the intensity of the sun, kudzu and other vines stick to cool walls with tuberous feet. Thin tunnels, dirt roads, graffiti misspelled in contrasted shade, occasional signposts with raised gold letters tell the names of minor battles, creeks, and only the palest of the dead.

- No wind to shake draped branches, the roads continue until red dirt obscures Google-able names. If you wander far enough, you might find the tendency to skim instead of dig becomes a burden felt along your shoulder blades.

- The origin of language, where granite uproots trees at sites of heavy violence — where lines press and remain. The cuts endured long after and were discovered, some years later, wrapped with twine and cast in cement.

- The foundation of houses along the ridgelines.

- Under the floorboards, the walls are clay and sweat like us. Regard the earth dismissing its structural employment as it slides down to the cement floor.

- Worms chew on loam. Wolves rut in wet leaves.

- A fence elongates peripheries here as cracked cement fades into dust. Each gash of construction reddens the lumber stacked nearby: Walmarts, motels, displaced burials. Creeks intimate against the bank hidden from road sun. A mess of fern and winged sumac. Around the bend, smoke tarries against the green. We cannot see heat in such heat, brush burnt in daylight. Apple trees, sumac, and the lingering from a limb of severed twine.

- I know simple words braid them, passed down through families too fragile to whisper any account damning their own. They inherit fracture along the thin veneer of false steel. To not shrug off but inhabit the place between strangling hands or a spit of land where blinding sun is less a cause for concern than the rising tide of a mob in advance. A scoff in another room.

- And even now, buildings compete with encroaching pinewood as cicadas hum regardless of larger bodies stalking below.

Absorptivity is at its highest at the resonance frequency, usually near or below 100 Hz.

"An example of proper sympathetic resonance is a windowpane rattling steadily at the very low powerful sound of a bus or truck engine going stationary. The rattling will usually occur at a higher harmonic of the sound made by the engine. As soon as the driver changes into gear the rattling will stop, often changing its rhythm before it stops altogether. Powerful sopranos bursting wineglasses fits in to the same category - sympathetic resonance at a distance."

-Arden Wilken

Failure of the original Tacoma Narrows Bridge

THE ELUSION ARTIST

My memory wavers —
an oscillation from sternum to feet.
The city expands to many times its size:

1.

The hotel room was sparse, almost windowless. A self-contained box of brown paintbrushes, knocked around for years, emptied of its contents, and yet, a residue. The lights were as if candles, haloing cheap Italian bedspreads. The wallpaper may have been peeling off around corners, reaching for a baser state.

The shape of a man sitting on a bed dominated the darker forms of chair and desk, long silhouettes held taut, demanding sinister repose. His edges retracted in that light, editing themselves for future inaccuracies, a constant wash, as if to decide on *this* width of arm the air must become less stale. Stability causes its own vibration.

More importantly, a suture — two mattresses, then one.

2.

"I want to sit on this bridge forever, on the edge of the world, each of us now someone else's horizon. The river Arno, and its tributaries: Sieve, Bisenzio, Era, Elsa, Pesa, and Pescia, converging."

To deflect. To refuse. To remember: that room, its eggshell glaze, and the shaded sun.

The shower wasn't long enough to commit me toward a means of escape. Grasped, I wanted to be released; once released, I found the confinement of a tiled, white bathroom entranced — each tile a beam.

I wrote on each tile with translucent soap. I sharpened the edge into a point. I rubbed the corners along grout, the underside of the faucet. I kneaded the shavings into the wooden cabinet to hide the excess. Luckily, like spit, soap disappears when worked.

Here, with this point, I drew a crouching figure, its head against a wall. Here, an attempted toe-touch. Here, a head, neck too thin to support it. I did this on the surface of every tile until it was daylight.

He chose when it was daylight.

3.
A streaming — inward.

4.
This is not an origin story. There was heat expanding on an unreflective surface, brick and stucco, rough — these hills were once volcanoes Aeneas built to shelter wolves. But that's a lie. False histories sometimes parade as coping mechanisms. Alchemical ancestry requires something more; in rejection the room does not fade. It must be made into other more complex exits.

A woman from Brazil once told me the mind creates containers our memories fill to figure solid narration. Manic, when pressurized, we feel an upward thrust and thus begin anew. The color of black-eyed susan vines, surplus on each surface. "Beau-ty," she said, "is effusive, the way molten rock sublimes." Broken mirrors leaned against eucalyptus, bark scoured by the weight. I can't remember how I found myself there, but I welcomed the palm reader's touch in the absence of closer bodies. Loneliness, another type of divination.

5.
I departed the thin hotel by means of old avenues lined with the tilt of buildings I couldn't read. Sequence, they say, retains a sense of form. I therefore moved forward, trying to forget that tiled wall I would meet in hallucination at each cornered turn. Yarn from the overflow of weekend markets lied tousled in gut-ters. Engorged, window boxes overhead dripped soil, anxiogen-ic to the point of breaking.

The trees were old, their height determined by arid soil and a high sun, size not governed by assiduous pruning. I imagined this. Then, like a bellowing whale, a bus engine cranked down the way, beached.

Rain marked leaves shivering in the throttled afternoon, and I breathed to let settle the disturbances surrounding me.

6.
I reached the edge of the sidewalk, an urban rumble, the end of limbs. The toe of my shoe left an imprint before my coming. Earth knows the sizes and weights of our bodies when it begs for a lie. Cement steeps in wet weather: under this — sand; and under this — fire.

A slab of pink pavement, its indentations filled with red chalk. Caves, inundated with surging seawater, act similarly.

7.
My walking became a method. Toward what, I didn't know, but I could hear the bus, still warming. "When does the structure dis-

the concomitant expression, somewhere
itself becoming.

[nauseous glare]

solve to let us move freely?" I thought, incessant with each step, the foot's vibration, and the shift in timber when encountering dirt in departure from cement. Crossing, curving around contour to hug and give form, a slight push, holding the landscape there, that slight rise. A hand waving in dissolution.

8.

Castor and Pollux were elephants in Paris eaten when Prussia gave siege.

9.

Until: a fence surrounding a forest. The woods are centuries old, a point of referral but also giving way. I should have been more circumspect arriving at such an unsettled square. Where streets align, a patch of leaves in trees where sight lines cut and multiply.

10.

A picnic afternoon was meant for a more public lawn. In the morning, the soil turns itself, incrementally regaining the form it had lost. This is the evidence of sculpture: Michelangelo's *Unfinished Slaves,* encased in stone, caught among different shades of shame. Holding, as if in protest, their own substance, that which makes them mobile, the soil that spills around his hesitant shoe, digging troughs at the foot of cypress, back erect in waiting, my feet slipping into mud.

11.

To search, in the multiplied light of two suns, the body that casts an irregular shadow and to welcome that body, its gradated hues of gray and pale yellow. Unlike the topiary garden, this forest is malignant. By day, refracted stains converge under the waste of leaves and sandwich wrappers. Later, one can still hear laughter and see a lying form, a figure reclined, as if moon-bathing to keep its skin opalescent, tissue paper pale, reading a folded newspaper.

12.

Then, one mattress. Or two — a suture edited for inaccuracies. The shape of a man, a constant wash. Sympathetic, his edges retraced. The width of an arm, retraced, and retraced, and — what could I do that, in doing, finally makes of his body an error?

13.

But my feet don't stop, and the shrubs, when lingering, become a menace. Frustration seeps like sunlight through trees unaware of the coordinated dance below. See, the dark figure, idyll-gazing? Its position pantomimes a water feature, a garden overrun and left to seed.

A PRISM OF DARK MATTER

Bone research —
desperate for logic to save me...

1.   Can a word emit light? Interrupting the initial beginning here, apologies must be made — but to whom? Those who would receive this light, if possible? Then please forgive.

1.1   At times, this text may feel like a tilted plane, registering in multiple parts of the body — a sway. It will work out, as long as the ominous doesn't take you away, off sideways, *forever.*

1.2   In other languages, *to wait* and *to hope* is the same word. Here, *to wait* and *to desire* are more closely aligned. As is *to fall in line.* As is *endocrine.*

WAIT: "What happens if we all waited at the same time? If there were no other sentient beings, time would no longer progress at all: it would be the end of time. Since the messiah will come at the end of time, the second coming of *Jesus Christ,* and the coming of the mahdi and of the Jewish messiah will happen when all mankind starts to wait genuinely." — Jalal Toufic[1]

— Robb Hannawacker[2]

2.　　In waiting, a figure slips into a lower level, a time extended, that is, rubbery, close to earth. This can be called *primal,* or, simply, wasteful.

2.1　　Not smoking, they are suspect, circumvented in all manner of behaviors.

2.2　　Instinct tells you to cut another path when the form looms ahead; conjure a reason to avoid; leave abruptly.

2.2.2　　It is OK to breathe. Shaking hands need more than objects they can grasp.

3.   Remember, the city is also a forest in the way you search.

3.1   One body illuminates the wilderness whose wildness is now lost, a virtual mime of *then* and *after then,* in constant reassemble.

"WILDNESS is the *death space* of significa-tion." — Michael Taussig[3]

ARCHITECTURE: "It is not in wandering that man takes to the street, but rather in submitting to the monotonous, fascinating, constantly *unrolling* band of asphalt. The synthesis of these twin terrors, however — monotonous wandering — is represented in the labyrinth." — Walter Benjamin[4]

FIGURATION: "The moment when emergent memory becomes *apparent, opaque*: we call this sympathetic resonance; immersed in a form we can recognize and attempt to grasp." — JH Phrydas[5]

4.   We seek encounters with this body even if not-present. Sometimes, when biking through paved-over cobblestone, the emptiness between buildings moves you: a slight push.

4.1   I remember cold sweat, wet bark and its smell of vanilla, a body riding next to mine, undone. This non-body walks down Dolores, the palm trees erecting a maze, failing in their attempt to *wall in*. Candles, mission-lit, red-stained windows, each surface an organ, caught mid-breath.

4.2   Intensity cutting street fog, we rent the back pew for a time.

4.3   Brevity not a fear of lingering.

4.3.1   Rather: in shadow, his opacity comes too close to real.

5.   We greet an interrogative evening: the trees and the street they line hold us accountable — then disappear in the overflow of light.

5.1   This light is *impossible,* penetrating desire.

5.4   The body, in losing gender becomes texture, that which begs for touch. Possibly this: a futile desire, enforced by the need for structure.

5.4.1   But in the striving and its fracture, "*every* body radiates."*

IMPOSSIBILITY: "My being subsists only from a supreme point of view which is precisely incompatible with my point of view. The perspective in which I fade away for my eyes restores me as a complete image for the unreal eye to which I deny all images. A complete image with reference to a world devoid of image which imagines me in the absence of any imaginable figure. The being of a nonbeing of which I am the infinitely small negation which it instigates as its profound harmony. In the night shall I become the universe?" — Maurice Blanchot[6]

7.   In cinemas, dust bunnies herd under rows of seats like flickering lights, escaped projections. He sometimes ducks into the dark when sunlight reminds him too much of the trees.

7.1   While watching, tiny shards fall from the ceiling, catching before hitting pale concrete.

7.1.1   In dangle, on hair-thin threads, he could tell the tilt of the earth by their perpendicular failure.

7.2   Can you stand the edge of afternoons; the way the sun hits faces squarely, obliterating contours in oversaturation?

7.2.1   A hesitance, when each walking figure mimics mobile blindness.

7.2.2   Half glittering, the rest immersed impenetrably.

8.   Night does not always tire in falling. Diurnal motions beg release, wandering streets to forget one's name, bricked up windows and shallow thresholds. Benches lose their function in darkness.

8.2   What if intention were merely a mark the stars trace on you in passing?

8.2.1   And yet, pavement growls and pulls, midnight blue not just a color.

ARCHITECTURE: "At the most we gaze at it in wonder, a kind of wonder which in itself is a form of dawning horror, for somehow we know by instinct that outsize buildings cast the shadow of their own destruction before them, and are designed from the first with an eye to their later existence as ruins." — W.G. Sebald[9]

9. On screens and billboards, a face. Battered, blinded, a hand's touch toward the mirror doubles the violence of aftermath. "Who are you?" it reads, the finger outlining the facial curve muddled in the glass. Passers-by stare forward in walking. Image before the injury: the not-yet-disfigured.

HAUNTOLOGY: "It affects and bereaves it in advance, like the ghost it will become, but this is precisely where haunting begins. And its time, and the untimeliness of its present, of its being 'out of joint.' To haunt does not mean to be present, and it is necessary to introduce haunting into the very construction of a concept. Of every concept, beginning with the concepts of being and time. That is what we would be calling here a hauntology. Ontology opposes it only in a movement of exorcism. Ontology is a conjuration." — Jacques Derrida[10]

9.1 To haunt is to displace time.

9.2 Heavenly bodies forget themselves in twirling.

10.   He attempts to avoid city stares when passing strangers in cramped traffic. A ruffled shoulder could mean a glance, a fall of fabric, and suddenly, thin hallways lead to bedrooms, every surface lit. Exposures maximize in waking, eyelids — church windows in glare. The face in haze a shade, and yet, what emerges, when creased with kohl, contour and muscle insistent, ready?

KOHL: "Instead of painting her lashes with kohl, he had blinded her eyes." — Nawal El Saadawi[11]

INTUITION: "More a 'shadow,' a 'swirling of dust' than a concrete and well-formed concept, intuition is an emergent and imprecise movement of simplicity that erupts by negating the old, resisting the temptations of intellect to understand the new in terms of the language and concepts of the old (and thus the durational in terms of the spatial)." — Elizabeth Grosz[12]

13.   Another way to say "invisible control." Another way to say "when the sun comes out from under clouds to light the trees at sunset." Affect before knowing we call *intuition*. When the line is walked, the line multiplies. When systems collapse, a woman whistles to herself under a chestnut tree, carving a lover's handprint into the soft bark.

14.   Purcell's *Dido and Aeneas* projects across rock walls, mossed and low: strings along the ferment, below waists, as if clinging in vibrato to dried leaves and ruddy earth. Rusted car parts and bolts mound among roots embraced: *Ah, Belinda* — an open window against the sidewalk lined with fake flowers, strangers wait in rows — *I am presst* — blinding sun, and the softer sun — *with torment* —

— Eadweard
Muybridge[13]

15.   They lose internal demarcation with backs immersed in shadow. Can you point to your corporeal territory, your beginning and end, loosely mapped by hair and nail? Across steep lines of tan and pale your contour gains composure. Photography, when sufficiently slowed down, reveals similarly. An arch in cartilage impresses the air in sympathy with prior forms: heads, in wavering. Heat — cast metal.

17.   You wait for bodies to collide: we call this *humanism,* and also *progress.* They never fail to be amused that trees grow where they left them. Dried thistle and bulrushes spread unevenly along the slopes of decaying ponds. A jungle heat follows, unbecoming to such a desiccative, pale topography.

FIGURATION: "These are the moments when something powerful — and dangerous is happening. Figuration is about resetting the stage for possible pasts and futures. Figuration is the mode of theory when the more 'normal' rhetorics of systematic critical analysis seem only to repeat and sustain our entrapment in the stories of the established disorders." — Donna Haraway[14]

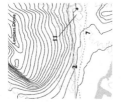

— us National Park Service[15]

20.   We fear a death we cannot grasp.

23.   What occurred first was only the means to ask and then break open the evening. Submerged in violet light squat figures mend themselves in moving.

23.1   Lines hover, encasing faces strained in action. They lift clay, smear mud and water along rough paths, set slabs.

23.2   Winter fails to happen here, augmented against redundant sunsets, violent light: as if *this* were reason enough, the build-up of heat, cicada-buzz, the path that, when followed, vanishes.

23.2.1   Around each bend, a human in transit, legs blending with brush.

FIGURE: "For an abstraction, the only way to gain solidity while remaining invisible is to contract a partnership with us, to keep the greater share for itself, and to allow us but an infinitesimal portion of visibility. And, it goes without saying, the full share of incrimination." — Jean Cocteau[16]

24.   Cement to dirt, this: reliant, heat no comfort, stares out windows *not enough.*

24.1   Head to toe in oscillation, where faces face, where body directs. A sideways glance, crab-like, holds on. Imprinted ground resembles the paths of fallen moths, irradiant residue.

VERTIGO: "The opposite, when walking through a valley of tight cliffs, looking up causes dizziness." — Bhanu Kapil[17]

24.2   Spiral movements more intuitive than straight shots. Think of weather patterns, wind through crevasse.

24.2.2 Think of snake prints in western sand dunes.

27.   And still, the roses.

THE ANIMAL: "The shadow escapes from the body like an animal we had been sheltering." — Gilles Deleuze[18]

28.1   His *geometrical force,* his *angle of light,* his *mobile yet rigorously immobile legs.*** He loses form in the waiting, soft lenses fog, diffusive.

28.1.1   To touch a body double — twin hues of thick light and ashen shadow beyond the pale.

28.2   Immanence turns to texture in being metonymically disfigured.

28.2.1   See: glass emerging from sand.

28.2.2   See: weathered bone, turning toward the swollen horizon.

28.3   Syndicate: rupture, and in catastrophe, bury each hand with the other.

29.   It is at the moment of dilation when seeing begins its own ascent toward *this vase she
made, its use in display.* Overgrown, a fenced
yard. The basement serves the purpose of attic
and looks on, accordingly. Figures motion beyond bougainvillea, tendrils sway in beckoning.
They hold similar objects, coralline and moss,
shells from the peninsula miles away.

29.1   Opening, the figures fall in, fence and
trellis, objects seen as active, there.

29.1.1 The pop of sound when reverberant.

29.3   From this angle, you are the view.

30.   Eye contact: a stare that runs along ears and throat. Veins in his arm mark reverence in lieu of tributary beauty, running strong until the trace recalls an effacement echoed by harsh sunlight in evening. The moment when angle trumps chiaroscuro, perspective destroyed by standing bodies, full of weight, in overflow.

30.1   This figure cuts a sheath from the sky, opening a fissure the color of night.

30.4   Focal, stars emanate through eyes onto skin, outside metered thinking.

— Giorgio de Chirico.
© 2019 Artists Rights
Society (ARS), New York/
SIAE, Rome [19]

32.   Still, figures mill near rose bushes, sunlight along petals, gilt selvage, a deeper navy
under leaves cast from a silver moon in transit.
They, in their stumble, caress discontinuities,
pleasures out of joint, grasping to remain, invisible. Silhouettes of windmills and metal cranes
hover, and even in crowded subways, faces skew,
the menace of architecture overhead, suspended.

REORIENT: "Phenomenology reminds us that spaces are not exterior to bodies; instead, spaces are like a second skin that unfolds in the folds of the body." — Sara Ahmed[20]

33.   And behind the tree I lean against: another figure, in shadow, excerpted, yet not so much *another*. We perceive bodies as not our own and treat them accordingly. But to reorient, as if that foot was mine, and mine, in standing on it, vanishes.

33.1   Circulation of bodies remains inconsistent with land grieving for more horizontal integration.

33.1.1   The moon and the sun just before eclipse throw shadows, bifurcating the body.

33.2   A prism of dark matter.

34.   Backs against bark, a hand fingers indentions, cracks between porous wood, calloused over, protecting delicate veins, as if to not fall off the edge of the earth, asymptotically. In entering, we make a promise in water. Egression fails to sever dense air between slight shifts of weight.

34.1   Small hands hold miniature organs viscous in the shadow of two pale streetlamps. Dripping, they mound and eddy as swamps begin to soak rough figures, emergent, lit from within.

34.2   Hands finger deeply in case a sharp tilt, a migration of wings, begin to bear.

martios							
Tabula afcedetis et de							
dies mensis	Bre minute	1	2	3	4	5	6
		7	8	9	10	11	12
		piscel	leo	agro	fcot	fagi	
		g	g	g	g	g	g
1	0 0	12	3	26	20	0	7
2	0 4	13	4	27	21	1	8
3	0 8	13	5	28	22	2	9
4	0 11	14	6	29	23	3	10
5	0 15	15	7	30	24	4	11
6	0 19	16	8	31	25	5	12
7	0 22	17	8	2	26	6	12
8	0 26	17	0	3	27	7	13
9	0 30	18	10	4	28	8	14
10	0 33	19	11	4	29	9	14
11	0 37	19	12	5	30	9	15
12	0 41	20	12	6	31	10	16

— Abraham Zacuto[21]

MIGRATION: "*Zugunruhe* is a German compound word consisting of *Zug* (move, migration) and *Unruhe* (anxiety, restlessness). In ethology it describes anxious behavior in migratory animals, especially in birds during the normal migration period. When these animals are enclosed, such as in an Emlen funnel, *Zugunruhe* serves to study the seasonal cycles of the migratory syndrome. *Zugunruhe* involves increased activity towards and after dusk with changes in the normal sleep pattern." — Wikipedia[22]

DESERT: "When there is nothing left, there will still be sand. There will still be the desert to conjugate the nothing." — Edmond Jabès[23]

36.   They do not believe me when I say: "there are two suns in our sky: one is pink, the other white." I have better luck when I whisper: "follow me, at dusk, and I will show you." I lead them toward, sidewalk, the intersection beyond, lines that flee as they draw near a deep ochre desert.

36.4   The Pre-Raphaelites clothe their bodies in persimmon, the color of longing, as you do now, gently, with sand. Others watch among the shaded copse, backs scraped with bark.

37.   We need a place of contact, thighs, sinu-
ous, the line drawn from heel to neck, arching
into inquiry. Touching paper leaves indentions
we construe as *now*, as: urgent. What arises in
the writing unravels at emergence, dissolves at
first touch.

37.1   Bodies behave likewise, inured to the
monolith of movement.

37.3   This is also a vanishing point, defying
itself when reached, lines that irradiate without
hope of convergence.

37.5   The hold that slips.

NOW: "There is a long present-time early life. Which really means that the action, or apparent source of origination — in the poem, and possibly in the sense of actual memory or life — is in the future." — Leslie Scalapino[24]

Endnotes

1 Jalal Toufic, *Undying Love, or Love Dies* (Susalito: Post-Apollo Press, 2002), 5.

2 Robb Hannawacker, *Mud flow patterns in Alaska,* digital photograph, http://www.goodfreephotos.com/.

3 Michael Taussig, *Shamanism, Colonialism, and the Wild Man: A Study in Terror and Healing* (Chicago: University of Chicago Press, 1987), 219.

4 Walter Benjamin, *The Arcades Project* (Cambridge: The Belknap Press of Harvard University Press, 2002), 519.

5 JH Phrydas, *Daybooks,* 2008–2013, unpublished notebook, author's collection.

6 Maurice Blanchot, *Thomas the Obscure,* trans. Robert Lamberton (New York: David Lewis, Inc., 1973), 106.

7 Virginia Woolf, "The Cinema," *The Nation and Athanaeum,* July 3, 1926, 314.

8 Francis Bacon and David Sylvester, *The Brutality of Fact: Interviews with Francis Bacon* (New York: Thames and Hudson, 1987), 56.

9 W.G. Sebald, *Austerlitz* (New York: Random House, 2001), 19.

10 Jacques Derrida, "What Is Ideology?" In *Specters of Marx, the State of the Debt, the Work of Mourning, & the New International,* trans. Peggy Kamuf (New York: Routledge, 1994), 161.

11 Nawal El Saadawi, *God Dies by the Nile,* trans. Sherif Hetata (London: Zed Books, 1985), chap. II.

12 Elizabeth Grosz, "Bergson, Deleuze and the Becoming of Unbecoming," *parallax journal* 11, no. 2 (2005): 8.

13 Eadweard Muybridge, *Animal Locomotion, Plate 532 (Movements of the hand, drawing a circle),* 1887, stamped on recto, 20" × 24".

14 Donna Haraway, "Ecce Homo, Ain't (Ar'n't) I a Woman, and Inappropriate/d Others: The Human in a Post-Humanist Landscape," in *The Haraway Reader* (New York: Routledge, 2004), 47.

15 "NPS Yosemite Tuolumne Meadows Map," US *National Park Service,* Restoration/cleanup by Matt Holly, January 17, 2017.

16 Jean Cocteau, *Diary of an Unknown,* trans. Jesse Browner (New York: Paragon House, 1988), 48.

17 Bhanu Kapil, class notes, 2013.

18 Gilles Deleuze, *Francis Bacon: The Logic of Sensation,* trans. Daniel W. Smith (Minneapolis: University of Minnesota, 2003), 20.

19 Giorgio de Chirico, *Mystery and Melancholy of a Street,* 1914, oil on canvas, private collection, Paris, France.
20 Sara Ahmed, *Queer Phenomenology: Orientations, Objects, Others* (Durham: Duke University Press, 2006), 9.
21 Abraham Zacuto, *Tabulae tabularum Celestium motuum sive Almanach perpetuum* (Leiria, Portugal: Abraham de Ortas, 1496).
22 *Wikipedia,* s.v. "Zugunruhe," https://en.wikipedia.org/wiki/Zugunruhe.
23 Edmond Jabès, *The Book of Questions: Volume 1,* trans. Rosemarie Waldrop (Middletown: Wesleyan University Press, 1991), 55.
24 Leslie Scalapino, "How Phenomena Appear to Unfold," in *How Phenomena Appear to Unfold* (Elmwood: Poets & Poets Press Inc., 1989), 109–10.

* Pierre Teilhard de Chardin, *The Phenomenon of Man,* trans. Bernard Wall (New York: Harper Perennial, 2008), 55.
** Jean Genet, *Funeral Rites,* trans. Bernard Frechtman (New York: Grove Press Inc., 1969), 83.

THE DELUSION ARTIST

*A fever-dream induced by
the workday dawning...*

I left early to avoid faces in morning traffic, seeing as it was a
type of holiday, window shoppers delighting in pre-dawn sales
while I stood at the mirror and looked at a dense set of teeth
caught between dotted lines that traced potentialities, I wondered if others noticed, crow's feet and eyebrows performing as
if tiny strings pulled from eaves, livening up, air from the heat
vent tightening the skin like an edifice, when contraction does
little to shift latent miscommunications, such as a tendon, pulled
taut at a 33-degree angle may send a mixed signal — of course I
know about release, when acetylcholine and Ca^{2+}, as if factory
settings, revert back to zero — smeared features and cropped
hair seemed out of place, sideburns buzzed amid fields of dark
stubble swept against a shorn chin, a smile equating to deep
purple or a decimal number, depending on whose authority you
attend, whose shoulders you stand on, and so I leaned closer
wishing I saw a mask or something marvelous, knowing each
species exerts its own rendition of disguise, in intrigue, as if ag-
grieved (a shifted letter) my eyes like markers slipped in and out
between signs: lines of emotive potential evoke a change since
there's a bred knowledge that wear might not always equal tear,

a soft wave, I breathed in, steeled myself for the day, the exit approaching, and I imagined the studio gates already open to mimic the sentiment of inclusion, such a joke, as if a universal trope could diminish a metaphor's intrinsic violence, my breath now discordant, its emphasis maneuvering again — these signs, why can't the mirror judge itself in me, for a flat surface, the aspect ratio need be half the height of its diameter for any symmetrical beauty to remain — and yet, I still see this lack, or how do you say, stasis, a fall out of time, my head divorced from my torso, an object of scrutiny from which the body reclines, in effect, a marginal sensation or type of site net, a topos of tiny pricks, if only I could be a shuffling of events, a force along the jawline setting teeth unnaturally on guard, rows of potential stalemate, a gaping shift, apertures reloading, I leaned closer to notice — oh, god — my teeth looked mirrored, in fact they're just shiny, glinting off the silver in front of me, the outside no different, in any case, like today, what it means to perform permuted *ad nauseam,* pores a bit more pronounced, in such a morning it could be worse than a trickle of remorse from a major late-night failure, replete in full, having mastered attempted side-eyes and overstated groping the other men seemed at ease, toes thick in water, ecstatic, the temperature fine, and even then whirring fans could not diminish the smell of fur and sticky floors, my eyes reflected these signs not lessened in attempted squints, still reticent to recede out my retinas' rear ends, those hanging bulbs and wet seats, to get this far ahead and leave the room of blue tiles, grey towels, an echo, perform the echo, go, and in going, remember that glance, the night undone, toiletries spilling over the edge of the sink, frozen there, a plastic waterfall of products, floor mats retaining footprints of the night, past bookshelves and photographs, a shrine to my mother, a basket of pale oranges, a wooden table in the center — what if each room only harbored one object, each house uncluttered, a synthesis of space and matter, soft threads against a massive frame, wooden beams, geometry, and a breeze when the door opened to exit, and entering see there the shine of polished chrome, a weight, two ropes in suspension into receding darkness, but not

to linger, exposed as-is, under halogens or natural light streaming through warehouse windows, a mark of reclamatory style, a
mission in penetrating *Homo oeconomicus* from behind, mete
punishment to live proximate to a produce stand, a cheese shop,
flower-engorged under sidewalk umbrellas, and mastery, outside of purpose, is merely pedantic, a place to hang a hat, as are
hooks along the wall, the next room, a wasted form, bone-heavy,
tight-lipped, a map in skin like matted fur of taxidermy left out
in the rain, I kept myself open to its folds — I'm not registering
so much as betraying an itemized catalogue, field of images, a
language, and what's worse, no sun in the eyes when the door is
opened, instead: studded streetlights paralleling sidewalks, tact-
less for such an early hour, the house dust spilling into the dirt
of the garden untended since the spring, I didn't have the temperament for feeding small items arranged for display, an excess
of energy, and what's more, dust on dirt creates an agreement,
soft patterns of beige on wet earth, a reminder of other maneu-
vers, the way hands slide over clay, the movement of fingers
along a crevice, deepening with each pass, each whorl of pressure: there, it gives, the surface retains marks, a force, what causes it, a language that intimates touch, casual or cruel, I measure
my level of calm by studying lines drawn on the wheel, the pot
or shard scoring the air around it, space holding weight as if it
too could drip over the edge, layers of dense and dried matter
covering the table, clogging up slits in the wood and metal hing-
es, plastic bags along the walls on floor-to-ceiling shelves a cel-
lular foundation, my basement studio and footsteps — stilettos,
leather boots, steel-toes, sneakers — along the floorboard overhead, waiting creates a din similar to most behaviors, but no, *my
studio,* the one whose doors left open by security makes a claim
to sentimentality, as if calling them "guards" raises the value of
what's within, as if a novelist were there, napping in the corner,
and often, as any other bureau lover would, I nailed chests-of-
drawers to walls and filled them with dirt and red kaolin, crum-
bling with any clumsy paw, as if to say, grid it, as if the compart-
ments themselves retained a drive for order, as if the method
wished nothing more than clean sheets, tightly knit, but, seeing

as the morning verged towards a tendency to crowd, instead of tending towards the bridge, like most mornings, I veered left to walk under the deep shadow of the bulwark, a massive umbrage I felt pressed the city concave, a shred of twigs and nets that, threaded through with random trash and plastic wire, weighed the center in nadir, and the streets appeared to fold, as if objects, there, descending, attached to every faint eminence and dip of cladding, covering "as-is" in rates and systems specific to such measurements, its dimensions implying a set of additions and completions building itself a vantage point, a means to rise and pierce perspective, that one rate impossible for the worker whose income depends on covering one's hands in mud and, starting from there, encasing: thick slabs, an ordered series, numbered markers leaning against walls and stuffed in corners, subdued edges never 90 degrees because of thin hairs along fingers, a loose grip on the handle, the curve begging attention, and this, over all things, a constant face-save, this curve over-arches and causes me to pause, seeing as I was, at the time, taking the circuitous route in search of larger bodies: as if to say, "in my small stature I retain some sort of value," in ratio — a sense of proportion, an anti-symmetric urge left out to tan on the lawn, as if multiple figures, a set of stones stuck with mud to a towering height, elongated limbs, a faded face covered by steel instruments patinated with rust — at this point, the front of buildings were contiguous enough, the slight chill of air kept my eyes open, glancing around corners paling as they filled, I hurried to pass the overgrown field before a stumble toward my workplace, a simple sidestep, a pretend lapse of memory as if caught in a muse, a play of light on the trees, a mix of color, impressionistic, and today only vomit could attain the field's precise hue, no chance for an HTML color code, although juxtaposing #FFEBCD or #E2A76F might suffice except for the potential to induce seizures, the vibration of coalescent putrid tints, the sidewalk before the cleaning trucks scour them with pressure washers, filling streets with mossy foam, opaline and smelling of sour milk, but, I have to admit, I find a shade of pleasure in the roil, and suddenly, the glint of a passing figure caught my eye, a firm stride, a willed deceleration, a fake phone check, a lean against the fence, a look back, a pause —

I consider such a moment a miniature event or broken time, a rift predisposed to elicit response, a glance or otherwise potential movement, and so I stopped across the street to tie my shoe, his foot on the lowest rung — a failed ladder along the field — as a flock of birds stood watching, knee-deep in grasses long turned brown, but this is not considered melancholic, the sun beginning to demarcate volume, a warmth and added suture, both sides of the flock departing in opposite directions unemotional as symbol or sign, merely objects in transit along urban crosshatch: corners and ruins, stale assemblies stacked on concrete rising up from the dirt, a cabinet below a street sign caught my eye as he turned to leave, the flock gone, a scene repeating, another glance, a figure among the brush in a halo of smoke, a breach accepted as reparations for the other's withdrawal, and after, I sought air, passing penitent mongers among the rough, sad cardboard of local sign-makers and purse peddlers, keystones burdened by the weight adding mystery to the myth, a tally kept of all the misses, fluctuations, engrossing methods of relation, a way to extend and in so doing rectify the sagging storefronts, constant shuffle, taut faces emboldened by law, a seated statue, a marble bronzed in commemoration of prior syntaxes, base raised above traffic in lieu of more precious accommodations, a reason to stand and cycle back, position toward a room of production, place-heavy, rudimentary, and still, wrought with accretions necessary for a vision, sight abstracted with an excess of aims, style disseminating graspable racist ideologies, a mention of rustic flavor amid tightly cut adages, serene hyperboles, an erection of castigated failures, mottled iron and chipped stoneware, a pile of indecency upended by malaise, the doors open for any random passer-by to peer in, this, an added bonus, debris another tool to live by, an ancient set of rules, a mark or curse to frame it, the body, until now, overwhelmed and suffocating — and yet continues along my sight, lines compel me like any other, all mystic notions reside in etched glass, neon lighting, since "The Psychic Is In" I can relax or forget to notice any preface to my motions, the time of day, the surge of bodies ascending from the subway, a stream of objects correlate to any type of mold, ekphrastic or otherwise, just as (in forgetting) doorknobs wear with each use, a minute impression surrounded by improv, unless a witness shifts everything, as if everything could contain itself rising, a call to choose, whether one watches the news or licks the salt off stamps, recollection rarely causes clarity outside of a stiffening of bones or finger twitch, even then to press out a form both readable and reasonable an undertaking in itself, disinter where the mounds are in evidence of deeper structures, and I finally felt the wind across my face, along my silver teeth: a preparatory grimace, unwilling to step amid the ruckus, I leaned against a wall, slid down hot brick, hands empty, knuckles resting along the sidewalk near dark splotches of gum, if only clay, then I could form a litany of objects, pyramids and tiny worms, like if finding the curtain's end would reveal the back-hidden, the way out, lines around the block, the air kept me seated across the road, studio doors agape, the in-and-out of traffic indiscriminately accelerating and slowing down, and the thought of standing up, reaching the table, finding the way in exhausted me, it's like an interchange might be necessary, onramps and exit signs, cordoned-off construction along the shoulders, green or blue signs, white words in Helvetica, street markings, a pull along the thighs, a shift of posture, looking changes, and then, as if on cue, a flood — a refusal washing over, suspended above, a merchant temperament offset by context to be left opaque and back to the wall, a figure in repose, when to walk is what's necessary, an impulse to move, and the movement itself, a push or resolve, and look, the windows are static, matted by the dust, clean edges still sharp, I scraped dirt from cracks and rolled them into balls, left them sitting in the sun, I had a tendency to touch everything proximate, an abundance, an accord lulling in its sympathy, a fade — towards rhythm and a lack of regard, figures in the windows across the way shared a certain timing, a way to relate: to stand and cross the street, ignoring faster objects and their aural reverberations, to try again, to get up, to enter the doorway, walk down the hall, descend the staircase, turn on the lights, stand at the table amid walls of piled earth, combine all energies in a gesture of control, and open — a soft resistance met me as I moved, clay amid clay molding figures, appendages, plastic temperaments, and contours, as if approaching what remained elusive in my morning prowl, stepping forward and shaping, the table a field, brown and dusted, strewn with untethered forms, points in a grid without context as lines left room for small breaths, sweat marking space through smudges, a heave, a glance, I set hands on the wooden board, my procedure replaced by the desire to feel the form give under duress, a release of energy from sedentary objects, set among the bags and piles ringed with tools, table covered in brown, and my clothes, and the floorboards, and in my surround: dust a layer on each surface, my feet making prints in heaps along the molding.

WILD HORSES OF MOURNING

I'm looking for someone —
a receding form:

Less a need for air than room to move, he left the
apartment for streets that expand on the horizon:
multiple vanishing points, wooden struts. Leather
sticks to my forearms while my heart, leaving the
hug of lungs, rises up my throat. *A flightless bird, a
blur of static caught in quick glide.* Clinging to stucco, the click of boots: a descent.

A city is also an extended plane in the way streets
move,

in the way bodies move through cities where neon lights mask subtler intentions. What do I remember? Pressed coffee through cheesecloth. The way he exits buildings. Words spoken through walls. A note. A node. But "this isn't a conversation," I say to the brocade. "It's a game of marks." His words made Xs across the whitewash, and mine, small like cuneiform. The rise and fall of breath scratched into plaster smudged by the feet of black flies.

Sometimes, stairways end in water.

I imagine grey ashes, contours of a face, how the photographer used filters of resonant reds and dark blues, intensifying his sides and multiplying. Likewise, architecture returns to its constituent parts: mud, dust, fibers, colorful piles.

The intensity of sunlight through venetian blinds

.

I sit, looking back. Beige, a stain on the morning, soaks into my arm. Thin ridges cross until a thicket wraps me, eyes toward the door. And through the door, a form against a park bench. Rising from the dunes, a live oak. Motionless, its bark etches a rough silence.

But where did these roads lead, ending in pale sand?

Figures line the dunes under a row of palms. Along the edge, drifts hold the streetlights distant. There, soil is more complex than sand where a mound's rise elicits firm skin, an arc of spine. One could imagine the cool of a hill dragged over them, *our houses, ordinary piles and bits of upright stationery,* immersed, like wet roots, in between clenched toes.

Turning, I lift a foot

and walk toward the shore along the saw palmetto:
figures stand with wild horses, holding reins invisible, each arm ending in a fist. Darker forms stand
in the oaks' shade, folding in the heat. The sun
makes the land swirl, a slight tug to the left, vertigo,
a polarized shine. Below the beach a floor emerges,
terrazzo — pale yellow and mauve — while sand, a
dull beige, forms piles that lengthen toward broken
oyster shells used frequently in local architecture.
Cement pools fill with seawater.

I open the door to catch a breeze.

Bodies lounge around the pool, now covered by beach-tea croton. The sound of waves, silent. Higher up, a fleck of clouds imitates the low tones of a sandstorm's approach. Slanting, the ground ebbs toward the call of waterfowl and salt collecting along the tips of Spanish moss.

Under oak, palmetto. In the dunes, wild horses. The figures are there, children in the way waves splash their feet and the glisten of palomino skin. On return, the figures remain, though the horses are now dark bay.

My head against hot leather.

I kick sand to expose the floor underneath: here,
mauve mixed with pale yellow. Who else loves the
way stones polish beneath the soil? And the pools
now empty. Low tide. Oak branches lower. Armadil-
los rustle sea oats along the eastern shore. Sand fleas
crawl from tiny cuts in the ground. I find a trunk
to lean against, bark coming off in small clumps
where my hands, in reaching, rip. Breathing in short
bursts, I lean toward sunlight coming through the
canopy in jagged lines among the palms.

My hands, a hot wall.

Light serrates through palmetto. In the shade, movements along the beach become hazy, over-saturated.

The expanse spaced fitfully with trees,

there is touch. I see him lie in the dunes. The cord-grass near his head oddly motionless. The only movement along the shore, a sandpiper sucking the soil. *"It's not soil,"* he says, seeing himself there: a mound, some grass, and a grey expanse that slashes the horizon.

With each turn another copse in view.

Pushed against the wall.

A breezeway.

And so, he leaves: his form down the metal stairs, the clank of boots. I remember the tips of steel along my back. I see a small, wet-footed child, a motionless figure on the edge of the haze. Its fingertips dip below the shore. I notice bodies waiting in the dunes and scattered clumps of cord-grass, lounging under oak near pools filling with saltwater. I watch the way light shifts as streets end in sand and know that under waves: terrazzo — mauve and pale yellow.

POSTFACE

On aesthetics,
facelessness,
and exposure

Look up! Astrology's one approach
To charting out the self
But the sky's too small—still there you are
At dusk, star by star.
— Bob Glück[1]

It is not necessary to hesitate at the insistence of the I.
— author's note

Origin harbors within it a sense of emphatic singularity. *This* is where I came from, what made me, *this* exact position of the stars. But what if we think of origin as a constant process? For instance, when we read, we receive words, imbibe them, and in the consumption — more an exchange than one-way flow — we can look to the positioning of the stars at that moment in relation to our bodies, *here, now.*

Within these stories is a type of witness: dirt, imprint, sidereal marking, sculpture, Michelangelo's prisoners, twin suns or orbs, the ambient noise of an engine off to the side. It's as if each paragraph has its own trajectory, pointing toward the final period. Placed together, in a series or grid, the propulsion of paragraphs may shift, an optical illusion, tugging us in a different direction each time we reach an end.

Where do we feel this movement? How can we pinpoint the overflow of etiology?

Gravity is one such layer of *what makes this possible.* As the period draws us — think of visual perspective — some painting techniques rely on the gravitational index of a single point. It can feel like falling or traveling along a steep ravine until: a stop. The point of illusion, vanishing into surface optics. This may pull you toward the unforeseen, strange body that itself may never arrive, or, if arriving, may reject. Think of iron filings, the way they scurry or assemble depending on polarity.

Julian Schnabel "gets" it, although he does not go far enough.

In his *Large Girls* series, Schnabel erases the eyes of young women, we say, painting over the depiction of sight, and yet...these are depictions of figures claimed to be women, the trust we give to an ability to recognize, our own ability to depict and pin down. These are figurations — they cannot see — looked at from the side, one would see layers of paint, the side of a canvas. We *project* a perceptive violence, Schnabel's blinding horizon lines. He does not go far enough because *he leaves our sight intact.* Thus, the figures remain recognizable. Subjected, the missing eyes become the vanishing point for our artistically controlled emotion.

In Schnabel's series, static concept retains itself without spillage. There is no *accumulation,* no *overflow.* Visual figuration, then, becomes only slightly aesthetically and politically volent in the way we receive. Our position as witness refracts through the method of approach. It gives less than we desire and leaving the viewer, themselves, flat.

An imperialist art that freezes as it figures.

What might happen in the act of witnessing multiple vanishing points, multiple tugs, when a work opens into a mutual exchange that exposes us as well as itself — an exposure to something unknown, unrecognizable, uncanny?

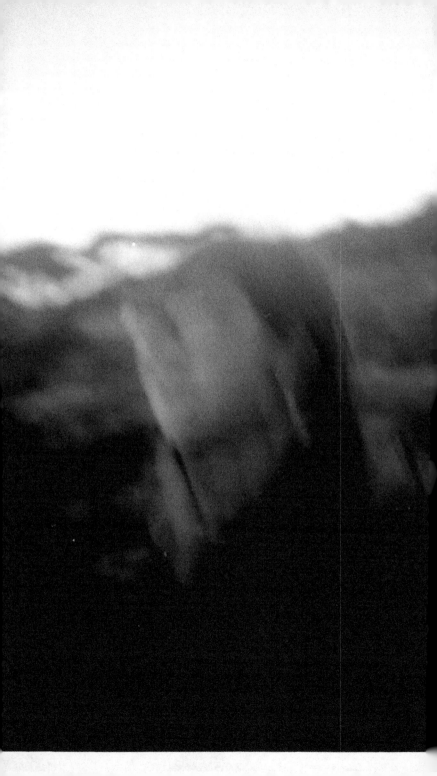

Can this exposure, for a bystander, be a type of origin? Oscillation — in revealing and hiding our bodies — enacts a gesture that accelerates through laying bare. Perversity is one kind of augmentation, where *losing* and *gaining* control becomes of political interest. Desire made vulnerable in the dearth of logical formality: raw, it surges.

And yet, this is *art* — what does this have to do with the rawness of exposing our bodies in a world prone to physical, psychical, and virtual violence?

Portraiture: the face locates identity when illumination reveals contours, curved lips, the length of eyelashes. Lighting, however, can become *too much* and obscure what is meant to showcase through over-exposure. Language, too, can open such a space when we demand access: a cheek to nuzzle or a chest to rest against.

A face obscured still breathes. And yet, in relation, our bodies react to disclosure viscerally, along the conduits of nerve and tissue. This has something to do with desire — non-productive desire — and the configurations this desire creates. Likewise, paragraphs constellate: stars form and seers give them names like *Virgo* and *Pleiades*.

In witness, the body of the reader as viewer is implicated in exchange. Color and line become gestures gleaned from the surface. Figuration becomes a mutual relation, when method determines outcome. If faceless, the figure may claim another type of value, one resistant to certain frames and intentions: sites for veneration as well as destruction. That which we do not recognize or understand quickly becomes suspect, skirting along potential retribution.

Can writing open a space of agency, re-territorializing both the soil and our bodies? Walking through a white space, signposts, paths — when the space blanks out, what happens to the figure, the body, those housed inside? Bared, we continue, shifting positions at each break.

These questions blur internal and external; implicit and explicit; representative and visceral life. These are questions of how *to figure* means *to value* as well as *to originate*. I will add one more term: *to orient*.

Reading positions us: at a table, sprawled on the couch, in the tub. Proactive passivity, where sensation informs and traces the edges of consciousness, our identities. What direction are you facing while reading this text? What direction is the figure facing when its face is obscured, unreadable?

When we stop attempting to understand, know, recognize, something else arises: prescriptive violence, or a tentative sense of touch. Our relationship to plants, rocks, objects, words as objects, as sculptural, sometimes tools but sometimes opaque to the point of uselessness — this relationship, *textural* instead of *textual*.

Uselessness: that which has the potential to become, on some subtle level, an anti-colonial gesture. To find agency in making our bodies unincorporated, such exposure opens a vulnerability — at the edge or high wall.

A vulnerable witness in artistic exchange. We cannot exorcise certain ghosts from the room, from the warmth of our beds. Standing on shoulders in dissipation, like mist. When each gesture spills over the matrix of the historical embedded in the social, back against a rough surface, its texture felt through skin. The ghosts are in the room.

How can we *know* if we cannot see?

Amid ghosts and the threat of physical and mental harm, *figuration* itself becomes a conduit for something other. Marlene Dumas and Zim Lin knows the whole face must be affected by obliterative pigments, lines, and oblique inks.

In reflection, in the failure of recognition, looking at Dumas's and Lim's portraits we are reminded of the self *as* present, oriented in the present, oscillating between a multiplicity of layers, planes of existence, or rather, through which the self ruptures or lies languid, indifferent to direct movement — an origin. In writing, the propulsion is a body propelled, positions shifting, recognitions obscured. Is this why figures constantly emerge from mud? Is this why bodies are torn from the night sky?

I want to witness impulses of desire through an anti-imperial art, where bodies seek contact outside of language and cognitive reasoning — as the incipient animal self — refracted through a self-reflective consciousness, a craft.

Like these portraits, the animal self resists being caught. As a viewer and reader, we are reminded as well as implicated, cascading the body in an axis of light that stretches from the stars and into the mud — to conduct that which lies underneath.

How can we open and become vulnerable to writing? The space of emergence, like someone speaking to you in the dark, and then, opening a door, you hear waves, the cry of sand birds, you smell salt on the air, the sun so bright you cannot see but clouded forms.

This bright space, the blinding white of an obliterated night. As the eyes adjust, we see a sequence as a constellation, a clustering, not yet named, continuously emerging, gesturing towards itself as a future moment, and event *about to begin*.

A writing that scans toward endless clusters of points on the horizon, the final periods littering a page as endings, as beginnings, each alone and tugging, points that orient as well as originate, wavering in and out of focus.

Endnotes

1   Robert Glück, "Wieners," in *Reader* (Venice: The Lapis Press, 1989), 6.

ON CLAY AND WRITING

THROBBING SYNTAX

Does clay have a throbbing vein?
— Bhanu Kapil[1]

In Krzysztof Kieślowski's film *Trois Couleurs: Rouge,* a man named Auguste sees his ex-lover at dinner with another man and hides from her subsequent pursuit of him across the street.[2] As the camera pans downward from her shouting form, we see Auguste holding his breath underneath her, vein throbbing.

To translate this cinematic pan onto paper, we must arrest that throb into stills, a Muybridgean scroll of images showing the rise and fall of a small shadow against Auguste's neck. To translate it into writing, something else must happen. A play-by-play description — *holding his breath, underneath her, vein throbbing* — like this scroll of images, morphs the affective resonance of the cinematic shot. We, as readers, must imagine what the words describe, closing the circuit between writing and movement, language and image. How does one write the poetry of a throbbing vein? Or put another way, can one write Auguste's pulse so the reader can feel it? See every beat of blood in his heightened sense of alert?

Imagine the beat of a line of poetry like its bloodline. Traditionally, the academy teaches students how to analyze rhythm through scansion — a system that wrings information from writing like a wet towel. Except here, what pours off the page registers in sound and rhythm, stressing the way we read — the way we sound. Institutionally, a normalized and recognizable pattern has feet and is mapped by dashes and accent marks. Think *iambic pentameter.* Think *"free" verse.*

What happens when tracking syllabic beats — when trying to find a pattern to hold onto — offers no smart-sounding name to contain or label it — any attempt at definition, in fact, falling, in suspension, away from the form, no repetition to hold onto? No pattern to pin down and discipline writing in a tidy line? Dactyls and spondees slip under the smooth dark surface of a different sea. Then, the surface of the body writing. It's funny how often I've heard co-workers and acquaintances wonder, aloud: "If it doesn't rhyme, what makes it poetry?" What then, does *poetry* even mean?

I cannot begin to explore an idea or feeling without coming, again and again, to this question that, on so many levels, is unanswerable. Because simply saying, "poetry is alchemical" doesn't help anyone feel better about the whole thing. Instead, my academically trained mind reaches to place the word next to others to find its meaning. The poetry of furniture. The poetry of a meadow overflowing with wildflowers. The poetry of your body, eyes watching the poetry of another bending over to touch your skin. What makes a *thing* poetic? If we can answer this question, we might be able to come closer to how poetry leans.

In *Rouge,* I thought I found it. That pulse in the neck of the ex-lover standing under the feet of the one that seeks him. How do I talk about it? What makes this, more than the lighting, the color, the feeling of the scene, what I call poetic?

Years ago, I wanted to write a text with a hatchet buried under the floorboards. This, I thought, was poetry. But I wondered, can the hatchet just sit — not a beating heart, mind you, or a body — with the reader standing or reclining above it, unaware? Or does it need marking, a thump or loose floorboard, signs of struggle, a latched cellar door? Must the floor beat? Can the hatchet remain completely unknown?

Nervous, I unlatch the cellar door. I fling it open to allow a harsh light to fall on the page, exposing the understory. I peer down.

This time, I find a room filled with clay.

|

I descend into the basement. Like many basements in Atlanta, some of the walls are made of concrete slabs, while others — where the house meets the rolling hillsides called, in this part of the country, *piedmont* — are raw exposed red clay. The basement of this writing intersects with clay in a similar way — dirt meeting a body willing to descend — in a messy type of exposure. Not an exposure like a body facing an approaching hurricane or side-eye, not like an exposure that abets state violence and control, but a subcutaneous one. The space between writing and clay is the space between our *self* and our *body*: thoughts and muscle, feelings and bone. I press a hand into the clay wall, its moist cool weight pressing back.

The power of that weight pressing back.

I pull a piece from the wall and begin to open it, then continue to fold. Open, fold, open, fold. Ridges form and sagging lines. Fingerprints leave marks like tiny topographies. Suddenly, I press the clay back into the wall, firmly, with intent. The object disappears — but not fully, the trace of my fingers along its surface, the thin layer against the wall, the warmth of worked clay against the cool of the underground slope. What I didn't intend a roughness, like any other.

a roughness like any other.

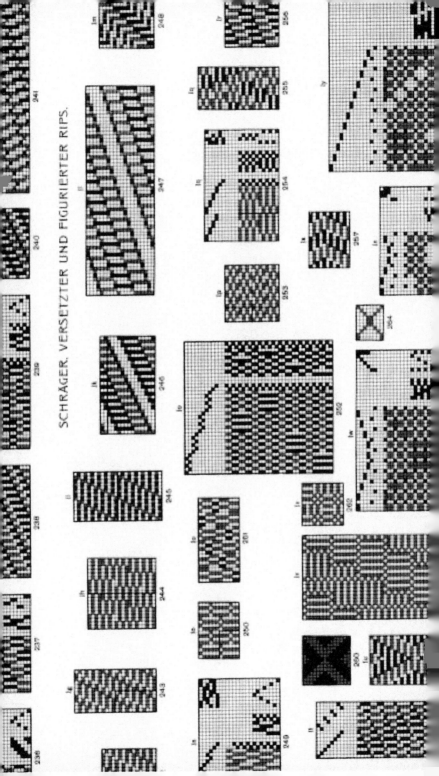

SCHRÄGER, VERSETZTER UND FIGURIERTER RIPS.

lies open in the way the bit of clay stares back, transformed yet still itself. I may have wanted to put it there, but its form is its own: it became what it wanted to be.

It's important to note that clay is never just a metaphor. Instead, impression holds the archive of the event, housing an index of ceramic imprint. A plastic give. Not to perfect some religious or allegorical proportionality, nor to evoke a culturally and historically specified beauty, the clay lengthens and extends beyond itself in an act that can be considered aggressive. A finger penetrates the surface to find more clay, its whorls a moist discourse we might read as if tea leaves at the end of an overdrawn and histrionic conversation.

This can be any tone, immersion an act unfamiliar regardless of its frequency. It might be enough to contour, but to depict with the intensity of locating and withholding against a contemporaneous embrace is something else entirely. Subtlety resides in friction, a long walk along the periphery. The form can easily detect nonchalance; like any substance accustomed to sitting along the edge of a basement corridor.

We can begin to think of syntax as a type of plasticity: clay-like in its tendency to mold and direct the line — a firm pressure point. Halts and starts, striations of the palm, encode a textural map whose key remains obscured. We might need a manual like Franz Donat's *Dictionnaire des Liages* — pages of gridded impact. To look at this texture, here, and proffer its semantic conclusion. Like tonal surfaces, shifts in hue register in another sector of the body — a getting caught, or the trap door feeling, an elision making the ground disappear.

|

In another angle of approach, the sentence becomes a queer body on a slab. Wires and nodes attempting a body scan. When we know more effective modes of acquisition: a walk in a garden; deep breathing; not a resistance to analysis but allowing for some type of mystical element. A striation — smooth muscle — easier to ignore, and the queer body itself that which we mold in and out of preconceived images and representations.

Take, for example, the comma that not only differentiates on a planar surface but correlatively supplies a quick chance to breathe, to re-collect oneself: a pivot point. As Bhanu Kapil writes:

> Syntax has the capacity to be subversive, to be very beautiful, to register an anti-colonial position: in this respect. I think of the semi-colon: how it faces backwards and is hooked, the very thing a content [shredded plastic] might be caught on. A content, that is, that might never appear in the document of place. Perhaps the poet's novel is a form that, in this sense, might be taken up [is] by writers of color, queer writers, writers who are thinking about the body in these other ways.[3]

Our comma, if excised, might be disregarded, claiming it makes no semantic variance, and yet, the lack of the hook, its twist, may cause any type of echoic forces with real consequences. Just as finalizing a ceramic sculpture with a fine-toothed comb, the glaze filling in crevice and ridge provide a sensory specificity. One that may remind the body of a lost memory, a conduit for materialization.

|

Particulate cements together in absentia of larger bodies. In effect, one major seam cutting through these strata is the notion of coming to the page as empty. Rather, we can see, like clay, that language is not formless until we bring our tactile tendencies to mold, draw, and assemble. Consider Levi R. Bryant's viewpoint:

> The problem is that *clay is not formless.* In fact, clay has quite an exquisite and determinate form at the molecular level. In-

deed, it even has form at the *molar* level as a heap of clay. It's just not the form that we would like it to have. What takes place between the wooden form and the clay is not an imposition of form on the *formless,* but an encounter *between* structured matters that generates a new structure as a result of the interplay of *both* of the matters interacting with one another. It is not an "active principle" (form) being imposed on a "passive principle" (matter) from without. Rather, both matters are structured, and both matters are simultaneously active and passive in relation to one another.[4]

We can say the same of language — in discreet parts, always structured, simultaneously active and passive — whose structure we inherit, predating us. It is no coincidence that multiple cultures have clay as the forming matter of the human body. Primal, we cover ourselves, whose transparent relative is language, and in writing, we bend in order to revitalize that arc.

Of course, we enforce a formal quality through a durational function. And yet, substance has a history, whether mathematical or molar, in temperature, hue, and context, before we arrive and cause a ruckus. Think of clefts and dens. Think of torn moss and quiet hooves. Movement has a vector, structured by position; the chiasmus holds as long as the gaze is returned — annulment no option when negative space incurs a type of solidity enacted by intense tension, tiny tools, broken wood. In such work, any fluctuation or turn of the head ruins a perfect angle, a smudged triangle of three distinct points:

A – Bring the tool to bear on the line: it severs, recombines, leaving a streak. Enough attention — a swarm of memories or conflicting emotions — can attenuate to the point of collapse. Emergent, a musical break. Typed and slow. Waiting, its own cohesive form in the thickness of silent resilience. It says, hold. Stand back and hurl it against the wall. Observe the wet stain it leaves as it slides to the floor.

B – Bring the wall to bear on the line: crushing certain phrases may make a claim for increased clarity, church windows molten and finally transparent. What can it tell you about more opaque situations, where goals are aligned more with the space within vessels than the cloths that buff them? A nick of a fingernail, a divot, our race and gender, our sexual desires begin a narrative the clay may hold or slough off in due time. Arc, it all arcs, in bare light or darkness, but to mold oneself an imago —

C – Bring the imago to bear on the line: clay is like language in the way it haptically transmits proximate registers. The hatchet we all carry, bury in mud, under intricately tiled floors, behind woodwork, beside heaps of nails and plastic sheets. See a silhouette slowly rise: an act and an event.

|

And the vein? A thin lode of crushed glass, as a reverberation of your arm lightning striking into sand.

Endnotes

1   Bhanu Kapil, personal correspondence, 2013.
2   Krzysztof Kieślowski, *Trois Couleurs: Rouge* (The Criterion Collection, 1994), DVD.
3   Bhanu Kapil, "A Conversation with Bhanu Kapil: The Poet's Novel," *Jacket2,* April 26, 2013, http://jacket2.org/commentary/conversation-bhanu-kapil.
4   Levi R. Bryant, "Hylomorphism: The Myth of Formlessness," *Larval Subjects,* April 13, 2012, https://larvalsubjects.wordpress.com/2012/04/13/hylomorphism-the-myth-of-formlessness/.

ACCRUAL LANGUAGE

1) What began as an interest in hue and texture began to accumulate into heaps on the coffee table. And what of these heaps? Can we locate desire here, a precursor to the libidinal thrill of definition? Filings and dust conglomerate and cause us pause as methods differ in more complex systems of assemblage — no need for direct patterning. Think of the way red silk drapery falls across a black and white polished floor.

2) In this century, the motive of exchange is always accrual. Even between cells and the motion of tendrils against a hot fence, to mimic and multiply. They've been doing it for millions of years, one says, and yet still, we focus with specific intensities. The mound, the hoard, the piling of acts that turns into knowledge. The epistemic trumps the somatic in an act of aggression: the underlayer of the human condition.

3) Take note: the rise of symbolic planes contains what should remain limitless.

4) We can read such planes as extensions of the body. The initial glance, repeated, invokes a spatial longing. A hand,

No. 763,870.

PATENTED JUNE 28,

W. H. FINLEY.
MUSIC TRANSPOSITION CHART.
APPLICATION FILED SEPT. 19, 1903.

NO MODEL.

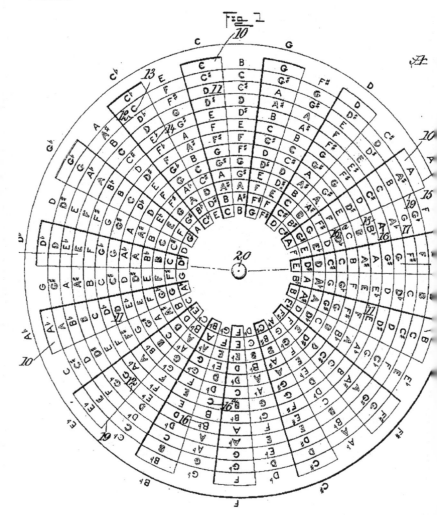

in shifting, solicits similarly, although impressed through a different register. In each instance a measure, a musical score, each line opening to another, proliferative. Five or six communicative paradigms occur simultaneously on the metro or in the locker room. He sees trivial movement while she feels a deep and sensitive invitation. Imagine transposing this bus ride from the key of G to A or D♭. This tonal shift can mark a depth in hue, a bleaching out of surface vibrations, just as a change in position enacts similar concurrencies.

4) The pile of sand becomes a figure for the impossibility of recognizing an approachable limit, even when the limit is desirous: handsome and wearing sweatpants. We lean toward the line when the line grants us a handhold, and the line falters, effaced. This is why they braid barricades into fabric, to keep the fleeing line at arm's length.

5) The sentence remains, as layer upon layer of objects in motion express an age and thus grow larger.

6) It may not be such a stretch to think that language, like paint, accumulates along the page, evoking texture: a plastic art. Verbal accretion retains its own singular attributes when compared with charcoal, clay, or alabaster. This is especially pronounced in the form of the sentence as linguistic build-up occurs in strands, a visual marker preconceived as linear, as (typically) longitudinal along the axis of the page. This string of elements, these particles of matter, add up, one way or another, to create something other than itself: a linguistic synergy, one that has the potential to exceed its grammatical structure. In the words of Andrea Spain, we can say these *extramaterial* and *extradiscursive* elements of language arise, emerge, become trackable when the accumulation of linguistic matter exacerbates its formal constraints — pushing against itself, it either opens or in-

volves like a hibernating snake, writhing to keep warm in its seasonal sleep.[1]

7) This type of accumulation occurs as overdetermined, amalgamated, un-codifiable: restless. As if paint dripping on the floor, rising as it dries. As if paper tacked to wooden beams, torn edges, smudged instructions, a longitudinal papier-mâché installation in the shed.

8) So, what are the *extramaterial* and *extradiscursive* elements in language? These elements may consist of patterns, textures, nonverbal communication through physical proximity, recursion, and prosody. Language, like paint and sculpture, acts on multiple hermeneutic planes. A text can be read for its content, its form, its syntax, its tone, its context, its somatic inflection (body narratives occurring within the line of the sentence, unconscious or otherwise). Each level can be mapped through Spain's take on the excessive — a linguistic excess as a site of dealing with memory and matter in the sentence.[2]

9) In the Abelian Sandpile Model, the slope builds up as grains of sand are randomly placed onto the pile, until the slope exceeds a specific threshold value at which time that site collapses. The original interest behind the model stemmed from the fact that it is attracted to its critical state, at which point the correlation length of the system and the correlation time of the system go to infinity. This contrasts with earlier examples of critical phenomena, such as the phase transitions between solid and liquid, or liquid and gas, where the critical point can only be reached by precise tuning (e.g., of temperature). Hence, in the sandpile model, they say that the criticality — its moment of crisis, so to speak — is self-organized, unforeseeable.[3]

10) Typical for most theories, the Abelian sandpile model is a play of thoughts. Always, it seems, grains of sand are

dropped from above, when in fact many piles accrete invisibly from beneath. An inverted hourglass retains its flow in relation to the center of the earth. In metaphor, this stream can access a variety of trajectories. Aas long as an object appears as a layer and becomes a deterrent, obstructing and allowing accretion to occur.

11) This occurrence acts simultaneously with larger and thus less obvious flows and subsequent obstructions. Think of money alongside a riverbank, stacks on stacks until buildings form and become resilient to future change. Both, here, rest on the slowness of speed, as if to grow or become larger, to collect one's own matter, must take time in order to insulate. Or rather, it's as if systems of integration take time to introduce and then knit the new to the original organism or crystal. It is difficult for us to know how to propel our being (what we will become) through anything other than analogy. In destruction, we learn to respect — we value the rare and unattainable. But rock is everywhere and therefore uninteresting as a representable subject, unless one crafts toward scarcity. Caught in the strain of the grey and darker grey.

12) Likewise, in drought, pastels surface to replace vibrancies. Transparency heightens accordingly, and accordingly, the beauty of those objects that preserve themselves gracefully in death. Think bull thistle, baby's breath, sumac, goldenrod, and roses: dried bouquets against a metal fence.

13) Once the sandpile model reaches its critical state there is no correlation between the system's response to a perturbation and the details of a perturbation. Generally, this means that dropping another grain of sand onto the pile may cause nothing to happen or it may cause the entire pile to collapse in a massive slide.[4]

13) The bouquets accumulate along an abandoned plot until, egregious, they disappear in the early dew.

14) Near this, a foundation left over from prior arrangements; an evening out of folds; vocal contour; the moment when outline and mien merge; containers; a swerve regaining its color; a bit of swell; all emotions left at the threshold; staircases; eyesight; streetlights; statuary along raised concrete; publicity; pedestrians, each face a mask; silent plots; value; acceleration; systemic fractures; a backdrop of facades and earth tones; fences wrapped with yarn; clay; grass in cracked blacktop; gift economies; baroque preferences; dried flowers; lines; limbs beginning to sway; machine parts; marginalia; elegiac street movements; cars; small birds; loitering bodies...

15) To loiter. To stand and breathe and sweat and look in all directions, a survey of a time whose duration can only be marked by exhaled breath — the beat of someone else's heart.

16) This comes closer to the surfeit of form whose accretion becomes of political interest. To collapse against an absence of definition, as color excesses form and bodies collide in the cacophony of broken-down names, as if cardboard lined with plastic, crushed and wet.

infinite skin

a form that resists. massive piles of concrete
that crush you in desire. to be crushed with
the weight of the real, dense love, the love
of flesh, of gravity's love for flesh brought
close, made to bear down.

surround, describe the interior,
the many points of entry.

light like a lingering

Endnotes

1   Andrea Spain, "Sensation and Art of Capture," *Trickhouse* 7, http://www.trickhouse.org/vol7/guestcurator/andreaspain.html
2   Spain.
3   Wikipedia, s.v. "Abelian sandpile model," last modified April 10, 2019, at 19:27 (UTC), https://en.wikipedia.org/wiki/Abelian_sandpile_model.
4   Ibid.

CAST MEMORY

The source of this illusion (for empty space, unenclosed, has actually no visible parts or shape) is the fundamental principle of sculptural volume: the semblance of organism.
— Susanne K. Langer[1]

In this book, figures keep disappearing — as if at the edge of the sea, the same sea where we started: *terminus*, the place of orientation, on the edge of the wild as well as the more structured wilderness, the forested city. Even topographies become objects via certain perspectives, a mind or root system glancing back toward the horizon. Emptied of affect, we begin to see this backward look as molds subtly incorporated into the objects they halo, a type of history. A spatialized conceptual practice can be theorized on the basis of phenomenal apparition, objects that retain a temporal quality at the intersection of absence and event, sticking to the object: a wooden guide.

Sculpture acts similarly. Let's take the physical process of lost wax casting as an allegory for spatial memory, the place where contours still hold along the texture of made objects, their place in space recognized, reverberant, continually active in the passivity of an object's nature. This proactive passivity transmits information via the space around, the spatial memory of that which made the object, the mold, the wax that existed at a prior moment in order to make the thing itself, in all its textural resonant energy.

As the cast falls away, it is retained in the texture, the shape, the contour of the object itself. Can we consider this a type of memory? Throughout this writing, the axial figure obsesses over other figures, these objects, hoping to remember how to remember by watching these objects enact memory at all times: simultaneous, in the present, bodily.

But if time accumulates and memory molds, where is the body?

Jean Genet knew this. In *Funeral Rites,* the body, now gone, in fact inflects the objects around the one that desires, the one who resists, so to speak, the beloved. Out of his mind, and thus out of his sight, the two are synonymous at this critical juncture of obsession:

> My hand was in his, but mine was four inches away from the hand of the image. Although it was impossible for me to dare live such a scene (for nobody — including him — would have understood what my respect meant) I had a right to want to. And whenever I was near an object that he had touched, my hand would move toward it but stay four inches away, so that things, being outlined by my gestures, seemed to be extraordinarily inflated, bristling with invisible rays, or enlarged by their metaphysical double, which I could at last feel with my fingers.[2]

An emergence that begins within the body becomes myriad, countlessly courting the line between conscious thought and unconscious desire, but, even more, cognitive knowledge and pre-cognitive sensation. A reverberative power expands the beloved body and its reach. Here, knowledge is immanent, a radiation whose origin is nothing more than the body and its sculptural position.

And yet, the body is a type of language, and, in writing, the body reflects its visceral confluences as we have seen in clay and accumulations of words, concepts, and syntaxes on the page. As the text becomes texture, and *technē* and technique arise through the poetics of the sentence, the spatial surround of writing emerges as an intrinsic aspect of its organismic semblance. Susanne K. Langer wrote of this surround in *Feeling and Form*. Sculptural volume, she says,

> is not a cubic measure, like the space in a box. It is more than the bulk of the figure; it is a space made visible, and is more than the area which the figure actually occupies. The tangible form as a complement of empty space that it absolutely commands, that is given with it and only with it, and is, in fact, part of the sculptural volume. The figure itself seems to have a sort of continuity with the emptiness around it, however much its solid masses may assert themselves as such. The void enfolds it, and the enfolding space has vital form as a continuation of the figure.[3]

This *spatial command* houses the *metaphysical double* that transfixes Genet, the emanation that he can *at last feel with [his] fingers*. Just as his text issues forth intensities of a textural drive, an interstitial longing.

This longing might have an anti-capitalist valence, albeit subtly, in the wings. The metaphysical doubling in virtual space may leave the object faceless — in effect, evoking a type of mis- or un-recognition, potentially leading to an inability to create exchange-value in the object whose visage is effaced in its own halo, its own memory. Like the loitering body which enacts a sort of wastefulness in its actions, the gesture of waiting, back against a chain link fence surrounding an abandoned plot of urban land — this can be seen as a slap in the face, or, more passively, a silent disavowal of capital hyper-productivity. Emanation, as spatial residue, recurs inadvertently, evinced via Spain's notions of *memory trace* and *a-signifying expression*.[4]

The turn from figuration to *technē* presents another interrogative landscape. Are these emanations, this spatial surround of the text, trackable as excess, or does this space, that which gives the *semblance of organism,* remain inherently manifest outside of epistemic analysis (i.e., a somatic or mystical remainder)? We may limit ourselves by thinking of memory as singly a cognitive act, when, in fact, the sensation of *enfolding space,* its *vital form as a continuation of the figure,* retains within itself accessible and inaccessible expressive features or elements.

So what, then, are these elements? What is the spatial command of a text?

One theory can be found in enunciation studies, which, in the 21st century, have shown how nonverbal elements in speaking reveal a sense of somatic identity that links to body memory, ancestral trauma, and pre-cognitive attributes. As social anthropologist Ellen Dissanayake points out in her investigations into "Prelinguistic and Preliterate Substrates of Poetic Narrative":

> Mother–infant interaction itself reminds us that linguistic theory, the philosophies of mind and language, and modern literary study [...] may forget that language as spoken also has crucial "oral" and paralinguistic properties. These are the "expressive" (sometimes called "prosodic") aspects of language — intonation, vocal contour, stress, volume, and other dynamic and expressive features that add emotional coloration and meaning to an utterance, allowing the hearer to infer and respond to a speaker's feelings, motives, and other states that may not be verbally expressed.[5]

Let us go further. Let us attempt to locate these *expressive features* of the utterance in written language as well, these visceral residues and somatic events. In a way that echoes Langer, these *extramaterial, extradiscursive* linguistic elements seem to have some sort of relationship with notions of sculptural qualities. Can we view these *aspects of language* in relation to object-dimensionality, textural qualities, a type of halo that surrounds as a layer of memory around matter?

The space of affect and pre-cognitive knowing: made possible by the resonant distance between your body and *this* —

Endnotes

1 Susanne K. Langer, *Feeling and Form: A Theory of Art* (New York: Charles Scribner's Sons, 1953), 88.

2 Jean Genet, *Funeral Rites,* trans. Bernard Frechtman (New York: Grove Press Inc., 1969), 83.

3 Langer, *Feeling and Form,* 88.

4 Andrea Spain, "Sensation and Art of Capture," *Trickhouse* 7, http://www.trickhouse.org/vol7/guestcurator/andreaspain.html.

5 Ellen Dissanayake, "Prelinguistic and Preliterate Substrates of Poetic Narrative," *Poetics Today* 32, no. 1 (2011), 69. DOI: 10.1215/03335372-1188185.

LIST OF FIGURES

1. JH Phrydas, *Attempts,* unpublished manuscript, 2006, author's collection, 7.
2. JH Phrydas, *Attempts,* unpublished manuscript, 2006, author's collection, 6.
3. JH Phrydas, *Attempts,* unpublished manuscript, 2006, author's collection, 11.
4. Arden Wilken, quoted in "Nikola Tesla, Sympathetic Resonance, Magnifying transmitter and the Wardenclyffe Tower," uploaded to Scribd by The Nikola Tesla Institute, accessed May 5, 2013, https://www.scribd.com/document/124380428/Nikola-Tesla-Sympathetic-Resonance-Magnifying-transmitter-and-the-Wardenclyffe-Tower, 18.
5. JH Phrydas, *Attempts,* unpublished manuscript, 2006, author's collection, 11 (modified).
6. Michelangelo, *Atlas Slave for the Julius Tomb,* 1520–23, marble, Galleria dell'Accademia, Florence, photographed by Jörg Bittner Unna, https://upload.wikimedia.org/wikipedia/commons/e/ee/%27Atlas_Slave%27_by_Michelangelo_-_JBU_02.jpg.
7. anoldent, "2000.09 Cumberland Is. Horse 2," *Flickr,* https://www.flickr.com/photos/anoldent/530468716.
8. JH Phrydas, *Bark,* 2004, gelatin silver print, 6" × 6", author's collection.

9. Julian Schnabel, *Untitled (Girl With No Eyes)*, 2001, oil and wax on canvas, 108" × 96".

10. Julian Schnabel, *Large Girl With No Eyes*, 2001, oil and wax on canvas, 162" × 148".

11. JH Phrydas, *Helem at Sutro Baths*, 2009, silver gelatin print, 6" × 6", author's collection.

12. Marlene Dumas, *Tulkarem*, 2002, ink wash on paper, 17¾" × 13¾", private collection.

13. Zin Lim, *Allegro No. D1*

14. Zin Lim, *Allegro No. 72*

15. Screenshot of Krzysztof Kieślowski, *Trois Couleurs: Rouge* (The Criterion Collection, 1994), DVD.

16. JH Phrydas, *Attempts*, unpublished manuscript, 2006, author's collection, 18.

17. JH Phrydas, *Attempts*, unpublished manuscript, 2006, author's collection, 18 (modified).

18. From Franz Donat, *Grosses Bindungs-Lexikon*, trans. Rudolf Teitscher (Vienna: A. Hartleben, 1904), 32.

19. JH Phrydas, *Sand Factory*, Valmont Rd., Boulder CO, 2013, digital photograph, author's collection.

20. W.H. Finley, *Music Transposition Chart*, US Patent 763,870, filed September 19, 1903, and issued June 28, 1904.

21. JH Phrydas, *Attempts*, unpublished manuscript, 2006, author's collection, 61.

Made in the USA
Las Vegas, NV
25 February 2021